CONTE

THANKS FOR YOUR PURCHASE

HOW TO TRAVEL ON A BUDGET

50+ BUDGET TRAVEL TIPS

AVENTURAS DE VIAJE

WARNINGS AND DISCLAIMERS

INTRODUCTION

There are four major costs when traveling. They are transport, accommodation, food, and sightseeing. This book covers ways to save money in each of these areas, and then some.

HOW TO BUY THE CHEAPEST FLIGHTS POSSIBLE

1. Be Flexible and Creative

The more flexible you are about when and who you fly with, and the more creative you can get with things like where you fly into, connecting flights, etc., the better the deal you'll get.

2. Buy in Advance

The earlier you book your flight, the cheaper it will be. Booking at least month in advance will get you the best deal. Planning this far ahead will also allow you the time to schedule activities around your travel, as opposed to the other way around.

3. Book Your Flight When it's Selling Cheap

The best time to book for your flight is on a Tuesday, at around 6:00 p.m. in the time zone where the airline company is located.

4. Book Your Flight from the Country You Will Be Flying From

Many airline sites let you choose your country. Choose the one you'll be flying from, which is not necessarily the one you're in. For example, if you're in the UK and want to book a ticket from Australia to Malaysia, choose Australia as your location.

If the airline you want to buy a ticket from doesn't offer the option of swapping countries, you may want to consider using a VPN so that its system thinks you're in the country. Two free VPNs you can try are the downloadable Tunnel Bear app:

https://www.tunnelbear.com

And the web-based Hola VPN Chrome extension:

https://chrome.google.com/webstore/detail/hola-free-vpn-proxy-unblo/gkojfkhlekighikafcpjkiklfbnlmeio?hl=en

5. Fly on a Tuesday or Thursday

Although it's not always the case, these are usually the cheapest days to fly on.

6. Fly Red-Eye Flights

Red-eye flights are those that run overnight. Not only are they usually cheaper, but you'll also save on accommodation.

7. Use Google Flights

Forget all the other airline comparison websites. Google Flights is the only one you need to check. It has one of largest collections of airlines, including low-cost carriers, which most other comparison websites don't have. It also has other comparison website deals, in case the flight path you want can't be created with one airline.

Finally, it's a good website for finding the cheapest flights if you don't have firm dates and/or if you don't know where you want to go yet.

www.Google.com/Flights

8. Check Your Flight on the Carrier's Website

Sometimes the price on the comparison website is higher than it would be if you booked it directly from the carrier.

9. Buy Multiple Flights Separately

If your flights have multiple stops, it may be cheaper for you to book them separately.

10. If You Book Separate Flights, Ensure You Have Enough Time to Change Flights

If you book separate flights and you miss your connection, most airlines will not reimburse you. Ensure you have enough time to check back in, which usually means going back through security, etc.

11. Ensure "Inconvenience Costs" Don't Outweigh Your Savings

Sometimes the reason your flight is so cheap is because the plane lands at an obscure airport or you arrive at some crazy time at night. You may lose all the money you saved by paying to get to where you need to go from the airport you land at, or having to spend a night at an overpriced hotel.

12. Ensure Inconvenience Itself Doesn't Outweigh Savings

Doing all the research and booking your own flights may only save you $50. Is that worth all the inconvenience of obscure airports, rechecking baggage, etc.? But every case is different (maybe you're saving $1,000), and only you can decide how much convenience is worth to you.

13. As Soon as You Find the Best Deal, Book It

The cheapest airfares don't stick around for very long. It's best to book your flight as soon as you can secure the best deal.

14. Check Ticket Prices a Day or Two Before You Leave

If ticket prices fall lower than they were at the time you bought them, the airline may refund or credit some of the difference. Many of the budget airlines won't, but it doesn't hurt to try.

15. Join a Frequent Flyer Program

This is especially true if you use the same carrier a lot, but don't let the accumulation of points be the reason you buy a particular ticket. Find the cheapest flight. If you happen to get points, great. It's a bonus.

THE CHEAPEST WAYS TO TRAVEL

16. Trains, Planes, or Automobiles

Apart from walking, buses are usually cheapest, then trains, then cars, and then planes. But this is not always the case. In the United States, for example, it is sometimes cheaper—and 10 times faster—to fly than it is to catch the Greyhound bus.

If there are three or four of you, then renting a car might be a smart option. If you're alone or in a couple, then riding on the back of a motorcycle will be cheaper (and often faster) than a taxi, and renting a motorbike is cheaper than renting a car in most places.

If you're a fan of train travel, check out www.Seat61.com for the routes and timetables of long-distance trains worldwide.

17. The Cheaper Option Depends On How Many There are inIn Your Party

If you're going solo, then a bus or train is usually your best choice, but if there are a few of you, then it's often cheaper or on par to split a taxi or private car, which will also get you there much faster.

TIPS FOR SAVING ON ACCOMMODATION

18. Fly Red-Eye Flights

OK, this tip is given twice. Red-eye flights are those that fly overnight, letting you avoid the need for a hotel. As a bonus, these flights are often cheaper.

19. Sleep at the Airport

If the connecting flight is less than 24 hours away, it may be worth sleeping at the airport, unless you want to have a look at the city your layover is in.

www.SleepinginAirports.net is a pretty good website to check out for this.

20. Couch Surfing

There is a whole community of couch surfers out there willing to give you a couch (or even a bed) to sleep in for free.

There are some horror stories, but I've done it a few times and have had nothing but good experiences, although I admit I'm more tolerant of others than most.

Visit www.Couchsurfing.org to learn more.

21. Rent a Car

I only do this if I am planning to rent a car anyway, but while you've got it you may as well sleep in it.

22. Camp

If you use a bit of imagination, you can find a place to pitch a tent for free almost anywhere you are. Take into consideration trespassing laws in the country you're in, and if all else fails, use a legitimate camping ground.

23. Squatting

If you're really desperate, abandoned buildings may be an option for a free night's shelter.

If you find an abandoned building and are considering staying in it, do a little recon first. Look for signs of life. The last thing you want is to be in someone else's squat—it could get a bit hairy.

There are often underground communities who know of communal squats, and these people are usually quite friendly and happy to help travelers. You can find them online, in chat rooms and Facebook groups, for example.

24. Pull an All-nighter

Leave your bag in a locker at the train station and party all night.

25. Get a Hostel or Cheap Hotel

Run a search at www.SFNonfictionBooks.com/HotelLook. That will search all the accommodation comparison websites to get you the very best deal.

www.SFNonficitionBooks.com/Booking is another one of my favorites.

26. Airbnb

www.SFNonfictionBooks.com/Airbnb is a site where home-owners can rent out their rooms, apartments, houses, etc. It's worth a look, especially for longer stays. Airbnb property owners often give discounts for stays longer than a week, and bigger discounts for stays over a month.

27. Online Classifieds

Look for short-term stay-share houses on www.Gum-Tree.com, www.CraigsList.com or a similar website, depending on what country you're in. If you're staying for more than a week or two, it's always works out cheaper to do this rather than stay in a hostel. You'll also get to meet locals, and have a kitchen, bathroom etc. Facebook groups are another good place to find long- and short-term rental properties.

28. Work for Food and Accommodation

Many people all around the world will give you free accom-modation, food, and sometimes even a little pocket money in exchange for help with farm work, housework, English tutoring, etc. To find them, check out www.Workaway.info.

Housesitting is another option. The work involved in this is usually taking care of pets, but there are sometimes other requirements.

There are quite a few housesitting websites you can look at. Some are better than others depending on where you want to housesit. Here are two of the more popular ones to get you started:

www.SFNonfictionBooks.com/Trusted-HouseSitters

www.Nomador.com

HOW TO FIND THE CHEAPEST MEAL

29. Cook for Yourself

It is always cheaper to shop at the supermarket and cook for yourself.

If your accommodation doesn't have a kitchen, then bread, fruit, and milk drinks are filling and require no cooking. If you have access to hot water, two-minute noodles are a winner. Baked beans and eggs are also easy to cook if you have access to a stove.

30. Eat Snacks

Chocolate bars, dried fruit, and nuts are always good to keep in your daypack.

They can keep you going for quite a while if you get stuck without food. They don't go off, need no cooking, store easily and give the body the energy it needs when you're on rations. Then you can just eat properly whenever you get the chance, concentrating on fresh fruit and vegetables. You should also take a multivitamin.

31. Don't Eat at Places with Table Menus

The places with menus on the table in book or pamphlet form are usually more expensive. A menu that is written on the board in plain sight is a good sign. It means the restaurant is not trying to hide the price, and since you can see it, you can know for sure what it is.

32. Eat Where There's Food on Display

Any place with meat hanging or a display case, or where they cook it in front of you, is one where the food is going to taste good and is usually cooked fresh. The exception is if they give you the food from the display cabinet at the end of the day.

33. Eat in Non-Tourist Areas

Or, if you are in a tourist area, eat in those places that are tucked away a little, down the alleyways, etc. If there are lots of locals, it's a good sign.

34. Eat Outside

Places that have only outside seating are usually cheaper, and those with no seating are always cheaper.

35. Avoid Buffets

They are only a good deal if you eat more than three or four plates of food, and only if they are all-you-can-eat buffets. Many are not, and are overpriced. The other thing to keep in mind is that if you're going to get sick from eating street food or foreign food, the buffet is what will do it.

36. Check out Zomato

www.Zomato.com is a handy website that will find you the type of restaurant you want in the area you're in.

SIGHTSEEING ON A BUDGET

37. Do Your Research

If you are in a place for a short amount of time and want to get the most out of it then it is definitely worth researching what you want to see. www.Wikitravel.org is a good starting point, as is www.TripAdvisor.com. These two sites will tell you the best tourist things to do, as well as a few things that are off the beaten track. They might also give you some money-saving tips for the area you are going to.

38. Go Off the Beaten Track

The non-tourist places are often cheap, if not free, and not nearly as crowded. They also usually provide a much more authentic experience of the country you are in.

39. Use Discount Coupons

Google search discount coupons for the sights you want to see, especially for big tourist attractions.

40. Groupon

www.Groupon.com is a website where people get together and buy things in bulk, therefore getting a cheaper rate.

41. Try Hop On/Off Sightseeing

Hop on/off sightseeing buses are available in most big cities. You pay a set fare, and they drive you around to all the major tourist attractions. You can get on and off as you please. There's often commentary as well, and the tour companies sometimes provide discounts on attractions.

The tickets last at least 24 hours, and sometimes a few days. They're a great way to see a big city with lots of attractions.

42. Use Public Transport

A huge cost when sightseeing is getting from one place to the other. With 10 minutes of internet research, or just by inquiring at your place of accommodation, you can find out how to get to a place the same way locals would. As a bonus, the first time you use the public transport in a new city is always an adventure.

Moovitapp.com is a great app for catching public transport. Google Maps can do it as well, but Moovit has options Google doesn't, and shows you extra information like whole bus or train routes.

43. Walk

Get a map with and mark out all the sights you want to see. Instead of catching buses, taxis etc. to each of them, walk.

44. Use GPS

It always surprises me how many people don't use GPS because they think it needs an internet connection. It doesn't!

The Google Maps app lets you download maps to your phone so you can use them offline.

45. Try Google Translate

Google Translate is another smartphone application that will save you money because you will never have to buy another phrasebook ever again. It's also free, and you can put a whole language on your phone so you can use it offline.

46. Get Lost

Don't worry about the maps—just walk around. Carry a business card or write the address of the place you're staying and just show it to a taxi driver when you want to go home.

47. Take a Bus to Nowhere

Just get on any bus and go. If you see somewhere that looks interesting, get off the bus. When you want to get back home, just take the same bus in the other direction.

48. Try Ride-Sharing

Use ride-sharing apps like Uber instead of taxis. There are many advantages besides it usually being cheaper. You can know the approximate fare before you get in, you don't need cash, and the ride will come to you.

Sometimes I use ride-sharing apps just to see what the approximate fare should be before getting in a local taxi.

Although Uber is common worldwide, many countries have their own versions (such as Grab in Asia or Bolt in East Africa). The local version is often cheaper than Uber and has more options, such as tuk-tuks and motorbikes.

MISCELLANEOUS MONEY SAVING TRAVEL TIPS

49. Buy Travel Insurance

Travel insurance is a must-have. You don't have to get all the bells and whistles (nor do I advise you to), but you want to be covered for major medical emergencies, especially if you like adventure travel or if you're going somewhere like the United States, where medical care is expensive.

Often, if you buy a ticket with your credit card, travel insurance is free, although the coverage may not be that good.

My personal favorite is Safety Wing:

www.SFNonfictionBooks.com/SafetyWing

50. Don't Use Travel Cards

Many banks offer travel cards so you can spend in local currencies, but almost all of them are a rip-off. They charge you conversion fees way above standard rates, as well as other fees.

A far better idea is to join a bank that refunds international ATM and transaction fees. If your country doesn't have a bank that offers this, use TransferWise instead.

Finally, if you ever get the choice to purchase something with your card (as opposed to cash) in either the local or your home currency, always choose the local currency. That way, your home bank, and not the payment processor, will choose the exchange rate. The one set by the processor is usually much higher.

www.SFNonfictionBooks.com/TransferWise

51. Get Medical Care While it's Cheap

Medical care in Western countries can be expensive. Consider getting your medical needs attended to and your checkups done while you're in a cheap country. You might save thousands of dollars.

52. Become a Travel Payouts Affiliate

Travel Payouts is a search engine for booking flights and accommodation. It also has other things like car rentals and tours, but flights and hotels are its main offering. It's the company that runs JetRadar and HotelLook.

The great thing about Travel Payouts is that anyone can become an affiliate and cash in on their own bookings. You don't even need a website like most affiliates, and there is no rule banning you from booking through your own affiliate link. In fact, the company encourages it.

Join up with www.SFNonfictionBooks.com/Travel-Payouts

53: Start a Travel-Blog Business

A travel blog is a lot of work, but you can get some pretty good benefits if you're a frequent traveler, including business tax breaks, sponsored accommodation, tours, gear, and affiliate income.

Be warned, though: a travel-blog business is not the same as just writing about what you did every day and posting some photos. To be successful you must run it like a business, because that is what it is.

If you are serious about starting a travel-blog business (or any blogging business), I highly recommend taking the Digital Nomad Wannabe Build Blog Freedom course:

www.SFNonfictionBooks.com/DNW-BBF

USEFUL LINKS

Flights

www.Google.com/Flights

www.FlightStats.com

www.BestOnwardTicket.com

Accommodation

www.SleepinginAirports.net

www.CouchSurfing.org

www.SFNonfictionBooks.com/HotelLook

www.SFNonfictionBooks.com/Booking

www.SFNonfictionBooks.com/Airbnb

www.GumTree.com

www.CraigsList.com

www.WorkAway.info

www.Nomador.com

www.SFNonfictionBooks.com/Trusted-HouseSitters

Food

www.Zomato.com

Sightseeing

www.Groupon.com

www.MoovitApp.com

Other

www.Seat61.com

www.SFNonfictionBooks.com/SafetyWing

www.SFNonfictionBooks.com/TransferWise

www.SFNonfictionBooks.com/Travel-Payouts

www.SFNonfictionBooks.com/DNW-BBF

BONUS REPORT
7 STEPS TO CREATE A LIFE OF TRAVEL

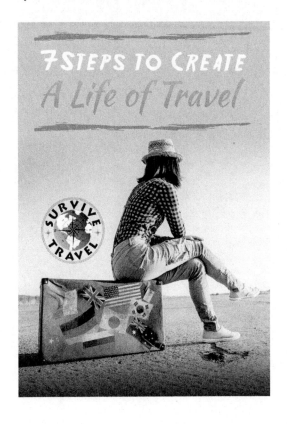

Welcome!

I'm Bert, creator of www.SurvivalFitnessPlan.com

I've been living a life of travel since 2003 and a life of freedom since 2015. What's the difference?

A life of travel means you're traveling, but you may still have to work or do other things you don't want to do.

A life of freedom means you're able to do the things you want, when you want, how you want. If what you choose to do is travel (like me) then great. But in reality, once you have a life of freedom, you can do whatever you want with your time.

In this report, I will guide you through the seven steps to creating a life of travel—and, for those of you who want to go further, a life of freedom as well.

Creating **only** a life of travel is faster than creating a life of freedom, but a life of freedom is much better. It's also possible to create a life of freedom while living a life of travel (this is what I did). You'll travel sooner, but it will take longer to achieve freedom. The choice is yours.

It took me several years from the day I decided to create a life of freedom to achieve that goal. I hope that by sharing what I've learned (and continue to learn), I'll help you do it much faster.

Well, that's it for my fluff talk. Let's get into it!

Note: Start each of the following steps in the order given. You don't have to complete the previous step before moving on to the next.

THE BASIC FORMULA FOR ACHIEVEMENT

This is not part of the seven steps to create a life of travel, but it's good to know for that, and for life in general.

Here is the basic formula for achieving anything in life:

1. Know what you want.
2. Make getting it your top priority.
3. Create a flexible plan to get it.
4. Carry out your plan with utmost persistence.

Well, we already know what you want: a life of travel! If you want something else, you can still use this guide, but you must be clear about what it is.

The second step in the formula is something you must do from within. Actually, if you want something bad enough, making it your top priority shouldn't be too difficult. You may have to become a little more selfish than you are at the moment, especially with your time.

The third step is what the bulk of this report is about. Most people think living a life of travel is all about money. While money does play a big part in it, there are other aspects as well. We will go through those shortly.

Take special note of the words "flexible plan" in step 3. Being flexible enough to change your plans is important for success.

You can change your plan without changing your end goal. Of course, changing your end goal is fine too.

The final step is another one you must do from within. This is the winner's mindset.

Do not give up. You have your plan; now follow it. Adjust your plan if you need to, but keep your eye on the prize— that is, on your end goal.

STEP ONE
GET ORGANIZED

You can read this report in less than 30 minutes, but to actually complete all the steps is going to take time.

You will need a scheduler/calendar and a notebook. I have Google Calendar for scheduling and Evernote for note taking. Both are free, and easy to use.

If you prefer old-school pen and paper, you can do that instead.

Take Action!

- Get yourself a scheduler/calendar and a notebook.

STEP TWO
BECOME A MINIMALIST

The word "minimalist" can conjure up images of people living in a house with nothing but a mattress on the floor. While downsizing your possessions is good, you don't have to be so drastic.

The truth is, being a minimalist is more of a mindset. Downsizing material possessions is only part of it. Learn to think like a minimalist and you will free yourself from all kinds of burdens.

Becoming a minimalist can be hard at first, but it's worth it. Your stress levels will drop and your happiness levels will increase.

It's also good training for when you start traveling. The less you have to carry around (physically and emotionally), the easier it will be.

Material Possessions

Get rid of your excess stuff. Sell it, give it away, use it for firewood, whatever—as long as you get it out of your life. I'm talking old clothes, knickknacks, fitness equipment, kitchen do-dads, etc.

Things you should keep:

- Items that could save your life (first-aid kits, fire extinguishers, etc.)
- Things you use often. The word "often" is relative.

Don't throw out your winter clothes because you
haven't worn them all summer.

- Very sentimental items. I mean things that would
  devastate you if you lost them. Pretend your house
  is on fire: What do you risk going back for?
- Items of appreciating value, like that rare, mint-
  condition basketball card. You can sell it if you
  want, but if you want to let the value rise a bit more,
  do that.

Take Action!

- Schedule a "spring cleaning" day **this** week. On that
  day, go through all your stuff and separate out all
  the things you will purge. If you have less time
  and/or lots of stuff, break this activity up into
  several sessions, focusing on one or two rooms
  a day.
- Once you have all your unwanted stuff in one spot,
  get rid of it. You can try selling anything of value
  online, and/or have a yard sale. Give whatever is left
  over away.
- I don't recommend forcing your family to
  participate in this. If they want to do it, that's great.
- Don't wait until you've gotten rid of everything;
  move onto the next part of this step!

People

Be selective about who you give your time to. Spend it with
people that make you feel good and offer encouragement,
those you love, and those who make you laugh.

If you're one of those people who feel like they have to please everyone, learn to say "No." True friends and family will stick around, and the rest will find someone else to rely on.

Once you know your true friends, be there for them. Help them when they're down, and they will do the same for you.

> When it comes to relationships, quality over quantity is the key.

Practice tolerance with others. Live and let live. Whatever other people are doing, if it's not directly affecting you or your loved ones, don't worry about it. There's no need to judge them or get angry, or annoyed.

Practicing tolerance will also be very helpful when you travel. There are many different people in the world. You'll have to adjust to the different cultures of the locals and other travelers alike.

Emotional Burdens

Whatever bad things have happened to you in the past, learn from them and let go.

Whoever has done wrong to you, forgive them. You don't have to reconcile, but be at peace in your heart.

Be honest with yourself, and with others. Trying to live a lie is a waste of time, and trying to keep track of lies is as well. Be honest about who you are, what you do, and what you say.

Take responsibility when you make mistakes. You will be free from guilt and people will respect you for it.

Sometimes white lies can keep the peace and make your life easier, but be wise when you use them.

Stop setting unrealistic goals and/or thinking you must get everything perfect.

Take Action!

- Have you promised your time to anyone that you know doesn't respect it? Are there any plans you've made that you don't want or need to follow through on? Whatever they are, cancel them. Don't lie about the reason, either. Tell whoever it is that you don't want to go and leave it at that.
- If you thought you didn't have time to minimize your possessions before, now you will!

STEP THREE
GET HEALTHY

There's nothing worse than getting sick on the road. Being generally healthy means you can experience more during your travels, too.

Living a healthy lifestyle is super important for living a life of freedom as well. Even if you have everything you want, you won't enjoy it if you're not healthy.

Being healthy is like saving up for retirement. The sooner you start, the better it will be for your future. On the flip side, it's never too late to start.

Nutrition

Healthy eating doesn't mean you have to go on a fancy diet or buy expensive "health foods." At the most basic level, you only need to follow one rule:

Make AT LEAST 50% of your diet whole foods.

What are whole foods? Here is a definition straight from Wikipedia:

"Whole foods are plant foods that are unprocessed and unrefined, or processed and refined as little as possible, before being consumed. Examples of whole foods include whole grains, tubers, legumes, fruits, vegetables."

As a bonus, eating a whole foods diet will cut your food bill —by quite a lot, in some cases.

Take Action!

- Throw out all the processed, refined-sugar filled foods in your fridge and pantry.
- Replace them with fresh whole foods.
- Visit www.SurvivalFitnessPlan.com/Nutrition-Guidelines for more tips on healthy eating.

Exercise

Exercise doesn't have to be a grueling 60-minute workout at the gym. My daily exercise routine only takes about 20 minutes a day, and 15 minutes of that is stretching!

If you want a no-equipment exercise that works the whole body, check out the SFP Super-Burpee. It's also perfect for hotel-room workouts.

www.SurvivalFitnessPlan.com/Daily-Conditioning-Workout

Do five of those, followed by the Survival Fitness Plan yoga routine, every morning and you're done.

www.SurvivalFitnessPlan.com/Beginner-Yoga-for-Flexibility-Strength

Take Action!

- Set aside at least 20 minutes each day for focused exercise, and do it. It's best if you do it at the same time every day.

Meditation

Ten minutes (or more) meditation a day can make a big improvement in your mental and emotional health.

An easy way to practice it is by doing Yoga Nidra. All you need to do is lie down and follow what the speaker says.

Of course, all types of meditation are good. Do it whatever way you want.

Take Action!

- Set aside at least ten minutes each day for meditation, and do it. It's best if you can make it at the same time every day. I like to do it immediately after my morning exercise.
- If you don't already have a preferred method of meditation, check out www.SurvivalFitnessPlan.com/Short-Mindfulness-Meditation-Exercises.
- To get even healthier, check out Sam Fury's book *Survival Fitness*. I use the lessons from this book every day.

www.SurvivalFitnessPlan.com/Survival-Fitness

STEP FOUR
LEARN HOW TO SURVIVE WITHOUT MONEY

Imagine you were traveling in an exotic country, and one day you got robbed. All your luggage, your credit cards, your cash, your passport—everything was gone. All you had left was the clothes you were wearing. And on top of that, that day was the last day you had booked in your hotel. Could you survive?

In fact, this can happen even when you're not on holiday. Societal collapse, even temporary, is getting more common all over the world. If a big storm hits and shuts your city down, what will you do?

At times like these, a little bit of knowledge goes a long way. Even if you never have to use these skills, knowing them frees your mind like you would not believe.

Train in subjects like survival and self-defense until you can say the following:

> Even if I was in the wilderness or an urban disaster with nothing but the clothes I was wearing, I would survive. I have the knowledge and skills to protect myself and my loved ones.

Once you can say this, not only will you be mentally free, you'll discover a new confidence inside of you. You'll also be able to use your skills to help others.

There are quite a few subjects that are helpful to know when it comes to survival. The following six are the most useful. Learn them first.

- Emergency first aid
- Escape and evasion
- Parkour
- Self-defense
- Water survival
- Wilderness survival

Take Action!

- Choose one of the six subjects listed that you have the most interest in learning.
- Head on over to www.SurvivalFitnessPlan.com and check out the free tutorials related to that subject.
- Once you have completed one subject, move onto the next one, then the next, and so on.
- Make it your goal to learn everything on the Survival Fitness Plan website. Once you do, you'll have the knowledge to survive almost anything.
- There is a lot of information on www.SurvivalFitnessPlan.com, and the site is growing. Don't get overwhelmed. Pick one skill to study. Learn it, then move on to the next.

STEP FIVE
ELIMINATE DEBT

Debt is a freedom-killer! If you're in it, do everything you can to get out of it. And if you have none, **never** get into it.

Note: You can still live a life of travel if you have debt (I did it for almost 10 years), but you will never truly be free unless you get rid of it.

There are three mini-steps in step five. Even if you're already 100% debt free, or you don't mind traveling with debt, you should still go through them.

If you're willing to travel with debt, at least pay off high-interest debts. Anything over 15% is high interest.

Reduce Your Expenses

When your goal is to reduce debt, you must reduce your expenses. Only pay for things that are necessary to maintain a basic standard of living: food, rent/mortgage, electricity, etc.

Luckily for you, being a minimalist is very conducive to this.

- Want to get a small loan to buy a better car than your neighbor? Don't do it!
- Want to join a phone contract so you can have the latest iPhone? Don't do it!
- Want to dip into your savings to buy that awesome new dress? Don't do it!

I'm not saying you can never do these things. Once you're out of debt, you can spend your surplus money on whatever you want. Until then, practice delayed gratification.

> *Delayed gratification is "resisting a smaller but more immediate reward in order to receive a larger or more enduring reward later." Definition via Wikipedia.

Take Action!

- Before reducing your expenses, you have to know what they are, so if you haven't got a budget yet, make one! Here's a free template you can download:

Note: This is an Excel file and will download straight to your computer.

www.MediaShower.com/img/2238/free%20budget%20template.xls

- Now that you know where your money is going, look for places you can reduce your spending. Adjust your budget to match your new expenses. If you need ideas, check out this article:

www.TheSimpleDollar.com/trimming-the-fat-forty-ways-to-reduce-your-monthly-required-spending

Create a Safety Net

If you were getting by before and now you have reduced your expenses, it means you have some spare money. Well, it's not spare. You need to save it. Save up until you have enough to last you at least six months on your new, reduced budget.

This way, even if you lose your job and all other means of income, you will have enough to live. Six months is plenty of time for you to figure out another source of money.

Do this **before** trying to pay off your debt. If lose your income and have no safety net, you will end up having to borrow money to make ends meet. This will increase your debt, which will end up costing you more in the long run, since you'll have to pay interest on it.

Take Action!

- Look at your budget. Take your total monthly expenses and multiply them by six. This is your goal.
- Open a new bank account. Get one with no fees. An online-only account works well. Online banks have fewer overhead costs, and pass the savings on to the customer (you).
- Put all your excess money into this account.
- Don't touch the money unless you have to. Pretend it is not even there. If you haven't eaten in two days, you can consider it.

Pay off Your Debt

You may have heard people talking about good debt and bad debt. For those of you that haven't, I'm not going to bother explaining it. When it comes to achieving a life of travel and/or freedom, all debt is bad debt.

If your goal is to become rich, then go research good debt and make your millions. But remember, "rich" and "free" are separate concepts, and as long as you have debt, you'll never be free.

> What if I already have large debts, like a car loan and/or mortgage?

A car loan is not an issue. If you bought a car that you couldn't afford to pay cash for, I have no sympathy for you.

Sell it, pay off the debt, and then buy something you can afford. Better still, use public transport. It's cheaper and better for the environment. Once you start your life of travel, you won't need a car anyway.

As for a mortgage, if you don't care about it and want to get to a life of travel and freedom as fast as possible, then sell your house. Use the money to pay off your debt. You might even have enough left over to jump-start your new life. If you want to keep the house, you'll fit into the "traveling with debt" category.

Take Action!

- Once you have your safety net, direct all your spare money toward eliminating your debt.
- If you have many debts, pay the minimum payment for each one. Concentrate all your spare money on whichever debt charges you the most interest.
- Pay the first one off, then move onto the next

highest-interest debt. Continue this until you have eliminated all your debts.

- Feel a massive burden off your shoulders once you're finally debt-free. Happy days!

Related Chapters:

- Become a minimalist

STEP SIX
WORK OUT THE COST OF TRAVEL

Once you are out of debt or have decided to travel with debt, you can start saving money for your life of travel. To do that, you must first figure out how much it is going to cost you.

Here's what I can tell you from personal experience.

- If you're a solo traveler who travels slowly and lives like a local, you can get by spending less than $50 a day in most countries. This includes buying flights to your next destination, paying for visas, sightseeing, etc.
- If you want to be safe, aim for $100 per day. This is enough to travel in more expensive countries, such as Australia and England.
- Add $30 per extra person per day. This is regardless of which country you are in.
- If you are traveling with debt, you must also add the cost of your repayments.

By traveling slowly and living like a local, I mean renting a place for at least a month at a time. It should be one with a kitchen, so you can cook. If you go out to eat, eat at local restaurants.

If you like to stay in expensive resorts, eat fine foods, and party all the time, it will cost you more. On the flip side, if you don't mind living in near squalor, you can do it for less.

Besides international flights, accommodation is the biggest expense for most travelers. When you rent a place for longer than a week, you'll often get a discount. When you use services like www.Airbnb.com and rent for a month or more, that discount can be up to 60% of the normal price.

If you plan to stay for a few months, then rent straight from the locals.

My usual drill in a new country is to choose a base and rent a small house or apartment for a couple of months. While there, I take my time exploring, while saving up for my next destination.

Take Action!

- Work out how much your preferred method of travel is going to cost you per day, week, and month.

STEP SEVEN
FINANCE YOUR LIFE OF TRAVEL

There are many ways in which you can finance a life of travel. Here are some examples.

Obtain a Large Sum of Money

By a large sum of money, I mean enough to cover your travels for the rest of your life. It could be an inheritance, winning the lottery, earning a large income and saving, etc.

Work and Save

This is the conventional way that people save up money to travel. It will work for a short vacation, a year-long sabbatical or more. You calculate how much the whole trip will cost and save up that amount. Unfortunately, for most people, using this method to save up enough for a life of travel is not practical. It will take too long, if you get there at all.

You can do it in short bursts. Save up enough for a trip, and then once the trip is over, go back to work and do it again. It's very doable, but not a life of travel.

Work and/or Volunteer Abroad

Depending on what country you are from, other countries will allow you to live and work in theirs. This is what I did for my first ten years or so on the road.

The downside of this approach is that you still have a job you have to go to. Often people get stuck, and all they end up doing is working in a different country. An upside is that you sometimes get free accommodation, which cuts a big expense.

Freelance/Work Online

If you have some kind of skill that you can use over the internet, such as web design, graphic design, teaching, or internet marketing, this is a good option. The more specialized your skill, the less competition you will have and the more you can charge.

You might even be lucky enough to have a job you can convince your boss to let you do "from home." This option can give you a pretty good life of travel. You will be able to go anywhere, as long as you can access the internet when you need it.

If you can find a job where you can make your own hours, you are getting pretty close to a life of freedom. Unfortunately, you will still have to answer to someone.

Importing/Exporting

This is one method that I have zero experience with, but want to try out once I have finished my other projects. I imagine it to be traveling the world finding items unique to a place. I would then sell them for profit in other countries.

Once you find a good item and the buyers for it, you can create ways to automate the process. This will create residual income.

Create an Online Business

Having your own online business will allow you to work whenever and from wherever you want. It also has the potential to create a very large income stream. Be careful though. If you don't set it up well a growing business take over your life. You'll have no time to travel!

If you do it right you will be well on your path to a life of freedom as well as a life of travel.

Take Action!

- Choose the way(s) you are going to finance your life of travel.
- If you're working for someone else, make sure the pay is enough to cover your living expenses.
- If you're working for yourself, make sure you're earning enough to cover your travel costs before you set off.

That's All!

Well, one more thing. These last few steps have a big focus on money. It is important to remember steps 2, 3, and 4.

Steps two, three, and four are the true key to freedom!

They will also keep you happy and safe during your adventures.

Right!

You are now equipped with the knowledge of how to create a life of travel.

Well, not completely.

There are lots of gaps you need to fill in, depending on the exact path you want to take.

Luckily, there is a ton of free information on the website www.SurvivalFitnessPlan.com.

BONUS CHAPTER
BECOMING FINANCIALLY FREE

You can have a life of travel without being financially free, but the same is not true for a life of freedom. As long as you're following the "work for money" system, you'll never be free.

To become financially free, you have three choices.

1. **Abandon the money system.** You will need to be self-sufficient and live off the land.
2. **Get a large amount of money**, enough to sustain you for the rest of your life.
3. **Create multiple streams of residual income.**

I'll assume you don't want to do number one, although it's not a bad thing. If you are interested in it, Sam Fury's *DIY Sustainable Home Projects* is a good place to start.

www.SFNonfictionBooks.com/DIY-Sustainable-Home-Projects

I'll also assume that you're not expecting a large inheritance within the next five years. And in case you didn't already know, planning to win the lottery is a bad plan.

This leaves you with option three.

How to Create Multiple Streams of Residual Income

A residual income is one that will keep paying you even after you stop working on it. It will pay you while you play golf, travel, and sleep. And when you die, as long as you set it up right, it will pay your family for generations to come.

You don't have to be rich to be financially free. You only need your residual income to be equal to or more than your expenses. Thanks to the internet, you can build residual income streams with little or no capital. Here is a summary of how to do it.

1. **Discover a passion** that you want to share with the world. It can be anything, but you should enjoy doing and/or learning about it.

2. **Create a way to share your passion with the world.** This is what you're going to use to make money. It must be something that, once created, doesn't need your attention. For example, giving live classes would not work (unless someone else gave them for you). Instead, consider writing a book, making videos, creating software or apps, etc.

3. **Spread your message to the world.** This is otherwise known as marketing, and is what will actually make you money.

4. **Use your profits to make ethical investments.** Ethical investments are ones in companies that do not have a negative impact on the world, but that focus on things like the environment, animal welfare, humanitarianism, etc. Backing ethical companies and products that make the world a better place is also a good way to give back.

5. **Repeat steps two, three, and four.** This is so you create multiple income streams. Not only will you have more income, but if one stream runs dry, you'll have backups.

Take Action!

- Choose a subject to build your residual income around. It should be something you're passionate about. Something you enjoy doing and/or learning about. Something you are happy to share with the world.
- Familiarize yourself with the different ways to create residual incomes. Pick one to begin with.
- Get your hands on a step-by-step plan for how to do it. If you search around, you might even find a good one for free.
- Follow the plan. Do at least one thing a day. Put each item on your calendar so you know what you need to do each day.
- Treat the income from your residual income streams like a business, because it is. Re-invest the money those streams generate to help it grow. You can treat whatever is left over as extra personal income.
- Continue to build more and different types of residual income streams. This will prevent you from getting bored. It will also safeguard you.
- If you want to increase your expenses, you need to increase your residual income. Only "upsize" your life when your residual income can cover it.

THANKS FOR READING

Dear reader,

Thank you for reading *How to Travel on a Budget*.

If you enjoyed this book, please leave a review where you bought it. It helps more than most people think.

Don't forget your FREE book chapters!

You will also be among the first to know of FREE review copies, discount offers, bonus content, and more.

Go to:

https://offers.SFNonfictionBooks.com/Free-Chapters

Thanks again for your support.

AUTHOR RECOMMENDATIONS

Teach Yourself to Meditate

Discover your inner peace, because this book has 160+ meditations
to choose from.

Get it now.

www.SFNonfictionBooks.com/Meditation-Workbook

Play in Perfect Harmony!

Discover how to express yourself through rhythm and notes,
because music theory doesn't have to be intimidating or tedious.

Get it now.

www.SFNonfictionBooks.com/Music-Theory-Beginners

ABOUT AVENTURAS

Aventuras has three passions: travel, writing, and self-improvement. She is also blessed (or cursed) with an insatiable thirst for general knowledge.

Combining these things, Miss Viaje spends her time exploring the world and learning. She takes what she discovers and shares it through her books.

www.SFNonfictionBooks.com

amazon.com/author/aventuras

goodreads.com/AventurasDeViaje

facebook.com/AuthorAventuras

instagram.com/AuthorAventuras

Printed in Great Britain
by Amazon

18795882R00037